NELLIE VS. ELIZABETH

Two Daredevil Journalists' Breakneck Race around the World

Written by Kate Hannigan   Illustrated by Rebecca Gibbon

CALKINS CREEK

AN IMPRINT OF ASTRA BOOKS FOR YOUNG READERS

New York

"Here is a race around the globe
between two young women
who make no pretense to athletics,
but who have been blessed with
indomitable pluck and
high intellectual endowments."

—*Atchison Daily Globe* (Atchison, Kansas),
Saturday, November 23, 1889

Eager and energetic, stunt reporter Nellie Bly loved to be in the thick of things—mud, muck, and all. Refined and dignified, magazine writer Elizabeth Bisland preferred the quiet company of a book.

Nellie was willing to go to outrageous extremes to catch a reader's attention.

Elizabeth was not.

One night Nellie tossed and turned, unable to come up with a story idea to give her editors. "I wish I was at the other end of the earth!"

That was it!

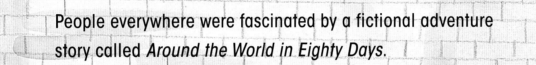

People everywhere were fascinated by a fictional adventure story called *Around the World in Eighty Days.*

Nellie's idea was to circle the globe—only she'd do it in just seventy-five!

Women are too delicate for adventures, scoffed her editors.

Sending a man—now that makes sense!

Nellie fumed, but her bosses soon realized stories about a woman traveling the world alone might make them a pile of money. When could Nellie set off?

"I can start this minute."

9:40 a.m.
November 14, 1889

Bounding onto a steamship and wearing a new dress—
her only outfit for the journey—

Nellie had barely left New York before she met her first challenge:

Seasickness!

6 p.m., November 14, 1889

Sitting in bed, nibbling toast and reading newspapers,
Elizabeth received a message from her editor.

He knew readers would devour stories about
Nellie Bly "girdling" the globe.

Would Elizabeth do it? In the opposite direction?

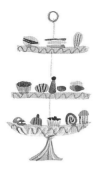

NO WAY! "I had fifty people invited to afternoon tea . . ."

But by evening, Elizabeth packed her bags and climbed aboard a train to California.

The race around the world was on!

Days 5 & 6

Elizabeth blazed 2,800 miles across America, reaching San Francisco bright-eyed and ahead of schedule—with time to ride cable cars and dine along the cliffs.

POWELL & MASON STs

411

"I wonder . . . how the coming generation that is to travel a hundred and a hundred and fifty miles an hour will bear the strain of it."

Nellie tumbled 3,000 miles over the Atlantic and staggered bleary-eyed onto England's shores. Leaping onto a train for London, there was no time to see the sights.

"As Nellie Bly has started round the world, the world had better pull down its blinds, or there will be no secrets the world round when she returns." —*Watertown* (NY) *Times*, **November 16, 1889**

Days 7 & 8

Poetry-loving Elizabeth plunged into the "sapphire and gold" Pacific Ocean.
Turning green with seasickness, she couldn't lift her pen for four days.

"Of her character it is only necessary to say that she started on the ten-weeks journey on six hours' notice. Sisters, think of that!" —*San Francisco Chronicle*, November 20, 1889

Boat, train, boat, train. Nellie worried a detour to the tiny French town of Amiens would cost her precious time. But shaking hands with *Around the World in Eighty Days* author Jules Verne made the delay worth it. She was determined to beat his book!

"It really is not to be believed that that little girl is going all alone around the world; why, she looks a mere child."
—Jules Verne quoted in *Morning Oregonian* (Portland, OR), December 1, 1889

Day 32

Elizabeth and Nellie were supposed to arrive in Hong Kong on the same day, but Nellie's ship ran late. The ticking clock pounded in her ears!

Stylish Elizabeth had time to explore busy markets. Buying up silk dresses, shoes, and kimonos, she was shocked to see women wearing pants. American ladies never donned trousers!

Stuck in Singapore, irritable Nellie shopped, too. Eventually she found the perfect souvenir—a monkey! "McGinty" became Nellie's curious, cranky travel companion for the rest of the journey.

"A cable dispatch announces the arrival of Miss Bisland at Hong Kong.
She sails tomorrow on the English mail steamer, three days ahead of the time
expected. At last accounts Nellie Bly was three days behind her time."
—*Daily Evening Bulletin* (San Francisco, CA), December 17, 1889

Day 36, around December 20, 1889

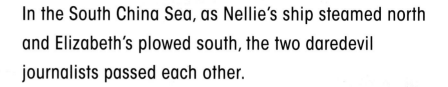

In the South China Sea, as Nellie's ship steamed north and Elizabeth's plowed south, the two daredevil journalists passed each other.

"'God speed!' cries every one to the two brave girls who, having chosen a career which for many years was occupied almost exclusively by men, are hurrying alone through foreign lands, with a view to a success which will rival that of many men of journalistic fame."
—Atchison (KS) *Daily Globe*, November 23, 1889

Day 39

Nellie's newspaper started a contest to guess her finishing time, and thousands of entries flooded the newsroom. The whole world seemed to be following the breakneck race between the two journalists!

Except one person . . .

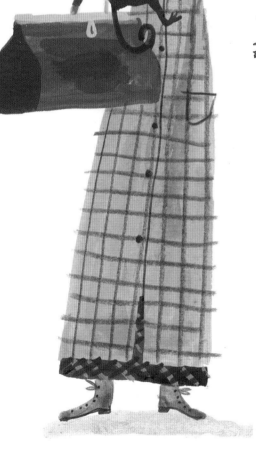

"I am running a race with Time," Nellie told a steamship agent in Hong Kong.

"Time?" he replied. "I don't think that's her name."

Nellie's jaw dropped. This was the first she'd heard of Elizabeth Bisland. Now she didn't just have to beat the clock. Nellie had to beat Elizabeth, too!

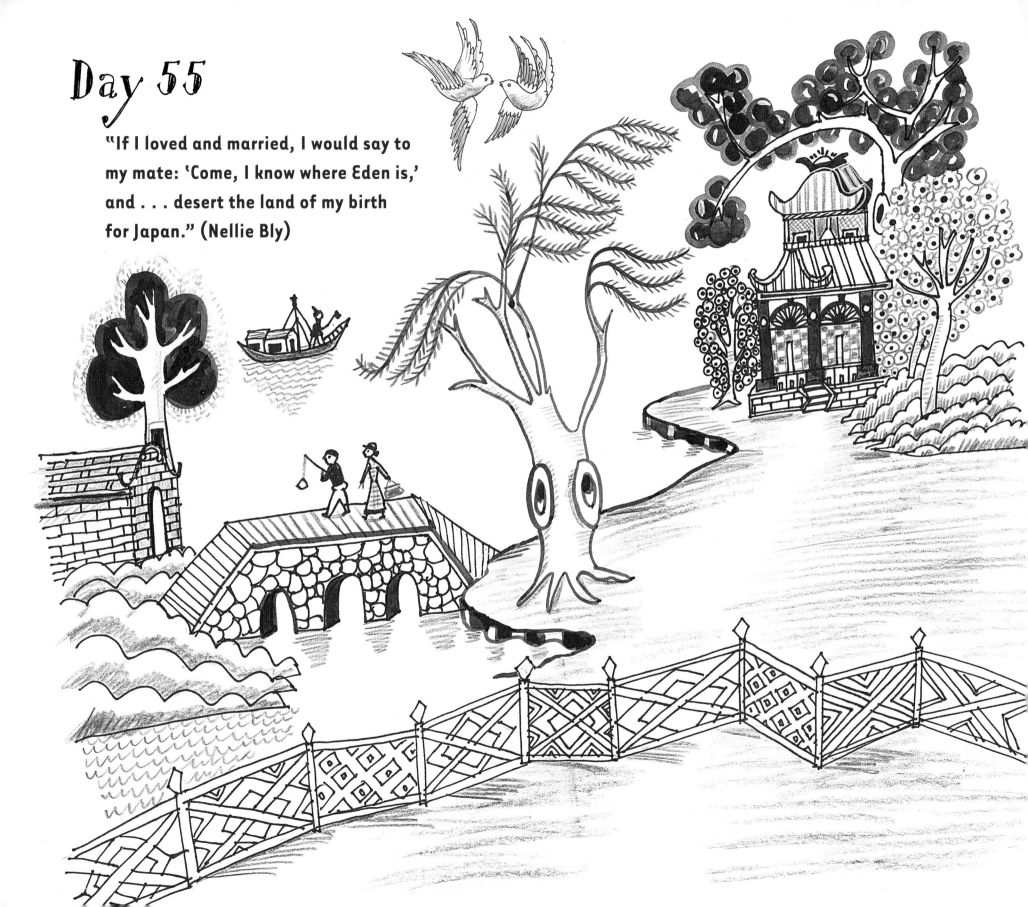

Day 55

"If I loved and married, I would say to my mate: 'Come, I know where Eden is,' and . . . desert the land of my birth for Japan." (Nellie Bly)

"I may never see this again, this world, where . . .
the light of night and of day have a new meaning;
where one is drenched and steeped in color and
perfume . . . " (Elizabeth Bisland)

Day 63

Nellie clung to the rails as Pacific storms battered the ship. Superstitious sailors blamed McGinty, wanting to throw him overboard. Twisting her ring to bring good luck, Nellie predicted she'd reach New York by January 26— just seventy-three days around the world!

Elizabeth glided across the Mediterranean, then sent a message to her editor tapping over the telegraph wires. She planned to catch a steamship off the coast of France, making her arrival date in New York . . . January 26!

The race was neck and neck!

Day 68

Nellie's boat bumped into San Francisco's harbor, and she scrambled to the railroad station.

But blizzards were dumping snow across the West, so her newspaper hired a special train to barrel through to Chicago.

"It was glorious! A ride worthy of a queen!"

Elizabeth bounded from her railcar near Paris and bumped into a travel agent. He delivered terrible news that her ship in Le Havre refused to wait. *You must make other plans,* he told her.

"The cause of this false information was never satisfactorily ascertained. It, however, succeeded in lengthening the voyage four days."

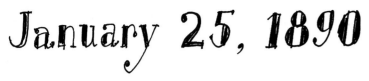

January 25, 1890

Nellie's train thundered over the finish line as cannons boomed and 10,000 well-wishers cheered and tossed flowers. Nellie had journeyed 25,000 miles and circled the globe in seventy-two days, six hours, and eleven minutes, the first person—man or woman—ever to accomplish such a feat!

"It is noteworthy that a goodly proportion of her admirers were themselves women. . . . Altogether it was a reception worthy of a princess."
—*North American* (Philadelphia, PA), January 27, 1890

Her ship hammered by surging waves and soaking rain, Elizabeth finally drifted into New York's harbor nearly one week later. She didn't celebrate her time of seventy-six days, sixteen hours, and forty-eight minutes. Though she beat the book's eighty days, Elizabeth hadn't beaten Nellie.

"I realized from the first that it was a hard fight between myself and Miss Bly, and, to say that I did my best to win, is simply to say that I never lost a moment from the time of my start."

So, who won? While crowds whooped for Nellie, and doubters said Elizabeth was tricked, the true winner was . . .

Everyone!

Because Nellie and Elizabeth made the wide world suddenly feel smaller. And they showed that women—whether outgoing or introverted, rough-edged or refined—could be just as curious, capable, and courageous as any man.

"People the world over have been taught that they are not so far apart as they had imagined, and that is a great lesson. You have set the whole world to thinking about it, and so have brought mankind nearer together."
—Mayor Orestes Cleveland of Jersey City, NJ, *Evening World*, January 25, 1890

AUTHOR'S NOTE

Nellie Bly's plaid coat and wool cap became recognized the world over.

Elizabeth Bisland's writing shows her love of poetry and literature.

When I worked in newspapers, I heard the same question over again: "So you want to be the next Nellie Bly?" Of course I did! Nellie represented daring and adventure, and today's journalists can thank her and Elizabeth Bisland for breaking newsroom barriers that previously had denied women entry.

Nellie's journalism career began in protest to articles about females, one of them headlined "What Are Girls Good For?" The writer declared that women and girls had little to offer society. Nellie suggested giving girls a chance. "Instead of gathering up the 'real smart young men' gather up the real smart girls, pull them out of the mire, give them a shove up the ladder of life . . ."

Born May 5, 1864, in Cochran's Mills, Pennsylvania, she was named Elizabeth Jane Cochran. She took on a pen name after turning in her first newspaper article. Because women at the time rarely wrote under their real names, one of her colleagues suggested a popular song at the time—"Nelly Bly." The spelling was changed to Nellie.

She went on to become one of the most daring "stunt reporters" of the time, posing as a chorus girl, a desperate mother willing to sell her baby, a deranged woman to get herself locked up in an insane asylum, and a factory worker.

Elizabeth Bisland was born February 11, 1861, in St. Mary Parish, Louisiana. Her journalism career began with a poem she'd written under the pen name B. L. R. Dane—to hide that she was a woman. After her identity was revealed, she was hired as a writer for a New Orleans newspaper and then moved to bigger publications like *Cosmopolitan* magazine under publisher John Brisben Walker, where she wrote essays and reviews.

While their personalities were different, their lives shared many similarities. They both arrived in New York in 1887, risking everything to chase their dreams. Elizabeth had only $50 to her name. Nellie's purse was stolen—along with all the money she had left in the world. Both Elizabeth and Nellie knew firsthand the challenges women faced trying to survive on their own. They would bring that deep concern for women and girls to their writing their whole lives.

When the two journalists raced around the globe, Nellie at age twenty-five and Elizabeth at twenty-eight, outgoing Nellie was by far the popular favorite. Unlike *Cosmopolitan*, which published only once per month, Nellie's newspaper the *New York World* was printed daily. Publisher Joseph Pulitzer whipped up readers' interest by offering an all-expenses-paid trip to Europe to whoever guessed Nellie's time. Nearly one million people sent in ballots, a staggering number for that era!

Once the race was over, Nellie and Elizabeth took very different paths. Nellie loved the attention and agreed to jump back on a train for a forty-city lecture tour. She basked in her stardom as parents named babies after her; animal lovers named their horses, dogs, even chickens in her honor; and a railroad called its fastest train the *Nellie Bly*. Children could play a Nellie Bly board game or read at night by a Nellie Bly lantern, women could wear Nellie Bly dresses and caps, and pantries were full of products bearing Nellie Bly's image—from baking soda to canned goods to medicines!

Elizabeth, always shunning the spotlight, escaped to a friend's home in England where she lived quietly for the next year, nearly forgotten.

Both women spent the rest of their lives with pens and pencils, busy authoring books, poetry, newspaper articles, and magazine reviews. But they will always be remembered for those seventy-six remarkable days, when they flung wide the doors to the world and took readers along with them.

Nellie lived until she was fifty-seven, dying of pneumonia in New York City in 1922. A simple stone at Woodlawn Cemetery marks her grave. Elizabeth also died of pneumonia, at age sixty-seven in 1929. She was laid to rest in the same cemetery, only a few steps from Nellie.

". . . And now, after six months, not a line has faded or grown dim. I can live back in it in every emotion, every impression, as though not an hour divided me from it. . . . It is well to have thus once really lived."
—Elizabeth Bisland, *Cosmopolitan*, September 1890

TIMELINE OF
WOMEN INVESTIGATIVE JOURNALISTS

1889: Nellie Bly and Elizabeth Bisland race around the world, writing their accounts for the *New York World* and *Cosmopolitan* magazine.

1892: Ida B. Wells investigates violence against African Americans for the *Free Speech and Headlight*, writing editorials on the lynching of black men that cause white mobs to ransack her press. A prominent crusader against lynching, Ida is not silenced by threats of violence.

Ida B. Wells in her early thirties, when she began her crusade for anti-lynching laws.

1902: Ida Tarbell's series of articles titled "The History of the Standard Oil Company" are published in *McClure's Magazine*, eventually leading to a U.S. Supreme Court decision to break Standard's "monopoly," or exclusive control, of the oil industry. An investigative reporting pioneer, Tarbell is credited with creating a new style of journalism referred to as "muckraking."

1931: Dorothy Thompson interviews Adolf Hitler, then leader of the National Socialist Party of Germany. Her writing and reporting on the rise of Nazism leads to her being kicked out of Germany in 1934. *Time* magazine calls Dorothy, a newspaper journalist and one of the few women in radio news, the "second most influential woman in America" after First Lady Eleanor Roosevelt.

Photojournalist Margaret Bourke-White wears flying gear while on assignment during WWII, 1943.

1931: Photographer Margaret Bourke-White publishes *Eyes on Russia*, considered the most extensive photographic account of the Soviet Union at that time. Among the first women to report on wars and the first female photographer to work on the front lines, in 1936 Margaret becomes the first female photojournalist for *Life* magazine. In 1941, she is the only foreign photographer in Moscow as the Nazis invade.

1937: Martha Gellhorn reports on the Spanish Civil War for *Collier's* magazine. She later works as a World War II correspondent on the front lines; her articles are collected in *The Face of War*. Martha is considered one of the greatest war correspondents of the twentieth century, reporting on most every major conflict that occurs in her sixty-year career.

Martha Gellhorn was one of the first female war correspondents. She was also a celebrated novelist.

1962: Science writer Rachel Carson publishes *Silent Spring* in *The New Yorker* magazine and later as a book, drawing attention to the dangers of pesticide use and helping to launch the modern environmental movement.

Rachel Carson holds her groundbreaking book *Silent Spring* in her home library, 1963.

1972: Frances FitzGerald publishes her account of the Vietnam War after reporting in Saigon for sixteen months. Appearing in *The New Yorker* magazine in installments, *Fire in the Lake* goes on to win the Pulitzer Prize and National Book Award.

1984: Jane Mayer becomes *The Wall Street Journal's* first female White House correspondent, travels overseas as a war correspondent, covers the fall of the Berlin Wall and collapse of the Soviet Union, and reports on the first war in the Persian Gulf.

1985: Television reporter Christiane Amanpour investigates Iran's politics and religion for CNN. She covers war and genocide in the Balkans, Africa, and Iraq, and interviews many world leaders. Her documentaries and television specials earn top broadcasting awards.

International correspondent Christiane Amanpour broadcasts while a group of reporters takes notes in 2004.

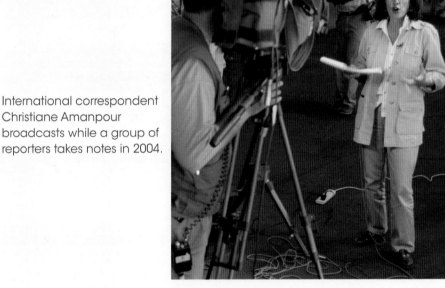

2001: Anabel Hernández breaks a news story in *Milenio* about the extravagance of Mexico's president and his misuse of public funds. She also writes about drug trafficking and Mexico's government officials and drug lords, putting her family and herself in danger. Anabel wins the 2012 Golden Pen of Freedom Award.

ILLUSTRATOR'S NOTE

Every new book starts with a new sketchbook. I read through the manuscript several times, scribbling notes, and sketching initial ideas.

With Nellie and Elizabeth, it was important to capture their individual personalities—the shape of their faces, their hairstyles, expressions, clothes sense, and even their taste in shoes! I will select the text where scenes jump out at me. I loved the moment when Nellie and Elizabeth are shopping, but for entirely different things.

Research is critical, not only for historical accuracy, but for inspiration, too. I will spend a good deal of time creating a digital scrapbook for future reference; old photographs, ephemera, old-fashioned catalogues, old ads—anything that will give me greater insight into the times.

There were plenty of images of Nellie Bly. Finding photographs of Elizabeth Bisland wasn't so easy, but this made it easier to create my own interpretations. I was in awe of Nellie traveling so light, something I've never been able to achieve. Can you imagine taking such a small bag on such a mammoth journey?

I wanted to capture Nellie and Elizabeth's sense of adventure, energy, inquisitiveness, and zest for life. I hope I did!

BIBLIOGRAPHY

All quotations used in the book can be found in the following sources marked with an asterisk (*).

BOOKS

Bankston, John. *Nellie Bly: Journalist.* New York: Chelsea House, 2011.

*Bisland, Elizabeth. *In Seven Stages: A Flying Trip Around the World.* New York: Harper & Brothers, 1891.

*Bly, Nellie. *Around the World in Seventy-Two Days.* New York: The Pictorial Weeklies Company, 1890.

Goodman, Matthew. *Eighty Days: Nellie Bly and Elizabeth Bisland's History-Making Race Around the World.* New York: Ballantine Books, 2013.

Krensky, Stephen. *Nellie Bly: A Name to Be Reckoned With.* New York: Aladdin, 2003.

Kroeger, Brooke. *Nellie Bly: Daredevil, Reporter, Feminist.* New York: Times Books, 1994.

NEWSPAPERS AND MAGAZINES

*Atchison (KS) *Daily Globe*, November 23, 1889

Cosmopolitan, September 1890, pp. 541–42

Daily Evening Bulletin (San Francisco, CA), December 17, 1889

Daily Picayune (New Orleans, LA), November 28, 1889

Evening World (New York), January 25, 1890

*Kokomo (IN) *Daily Gazette Tribune*, January 31, 1890

Morning Oregonian (Portland, OR), December 1, 1889

*New Brunswick (NJ) *Daily Home News*, November 21, 1889

New York World, November 15, 1889

North American (Philadelphia, PA), January 27, 1890

San Francisco Chronicle, November 20, 1889

Washington Post, November 16, 1889

*Watertown (NY) *Times*, November 16, 1889

Wisconsin State Register (Portage, WI), November 30, 1889

Yenowine's News (Milwaukee, WI), February 2, 1890

Library of Congress. "Chronicling America." chroniclingamerica.loc.gov/lccn/sn83030193/1890-01-25/ed-4/seq-1.pdf

Website active at time of publication

ACKNOWLEDGMENTS

Thank you to Dr. Arlisha R. Norwood, professor of United States history and women's history, for her keen eye and insight. And to Bon and Shoko Koizumi of the Lafcadio Hearn Memorial Museum in Matsue, Shimane Prefecture, Japan, for providing the photograph of Elizabeth Bisland.

PICTURE CREDITS

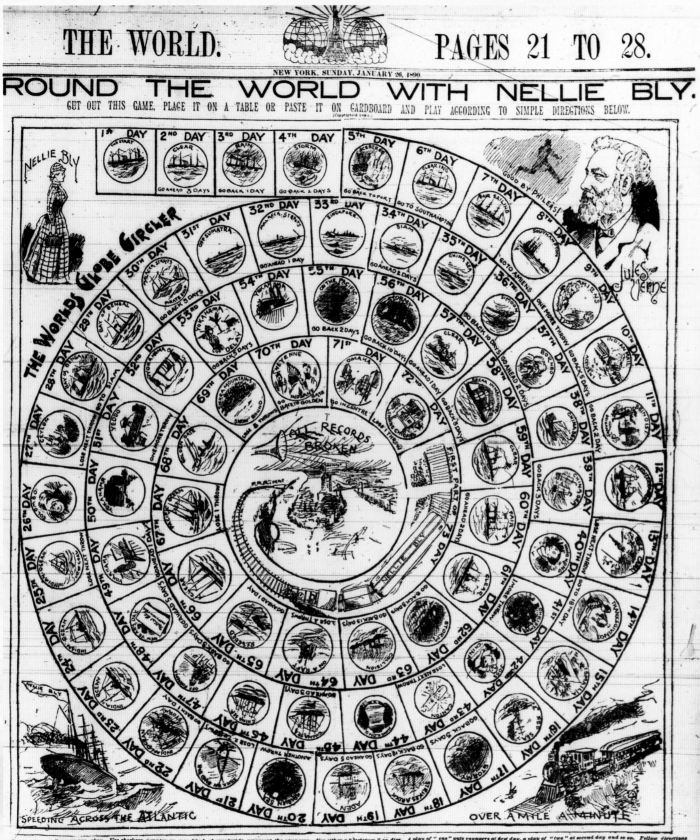

On January 26, 1890, Nellie Bly's *New York World* newspaper ran this Round the World Game highlighting the 72-day trip.

For Elena Valussi & Jennifer Fleming, intrepid globetrotters —*KH*

For my sister Lindsay —*RG*

For information about permission to reproduce selections
from this book, please contact permissions@astrapublishinghouse.com.

Calkins Creek
An imprint of Astra Books for Young Readers,
a division of Astra Publishing House
calkinscreekbooks.com
Printed in China

ISBN: 978-1-68437-377-2 (hc)
ISBN: 978-1-63592-554-8 (eBook)
Library of Congress Control Number: 2021906402

First edition
10 9 8 7 6 5 4 3 2 1

Design by Barbara Grzeslo
The text is set in ITC Avant Garde Gothic.
The quotes are set in Tarzana Narrow Bold.
Art done with acrylic inks & colored pencil on acid-free cartridge paper.